Reflections On a Crystal Wind

The Poetry of Michael Graves

Hugo House Publishers, Ltd.

Reflections on a Crystal Wind: The Poetry of Michael Graves

©2016. Michael Graves. All Rights Reserved.
No part of this book may be reproduced or transmitted in any form or by any means, electronic or mechanical, including photocopying, recording, or by any information storage and retrieval system without written permission of the publisher.

ISBN: 978-1-936449-73-6
Library of Congress Control Number: 2016937541

Cover Design: Dali Bahat

Interior Layout: Ronda Taylor, www.taylorbydesign.com

Hugo House Publishers, Ltd.
Denver, Colorado
Austin, Texas
www.HugoHousePublishers.com

This book is dedicated to Holley, who saved my life. And who has put up with her poet-husband through it all. And to Jim Doyle—poet, and a professor of mine at the University of Northern Colorado—who gave me perspective regarding my poetry at a time when I needed it. And to Carole Eddington, poet—who gave me the nudge that got all of this re-started.

My deepest gratitude to Bennett Fontenot, DDS, and to Don Dewsnap; without whose help and generous support it would have taken far longer to get this book published. And to Patricia Ross, my editor.

Cover designed by Dali Bahat, with my thanks.

Contents

Snacking on Bukowski 1
The View from the Lighthouse 3
Decision 6
Steinbeck's Ghost 8
Beatitudes 10
Tonight 12
Like Hemingway On The Streets Of Spain 13
The River 17
The Sea 19
The Air. 21
Vengeance 'lex talionis' (For the suicide bombers) 22
Taking Off My Watch 24
The Life of Dreams 25
Friendship 27
Mountaineer (to Jaxon) 29
Dreams—(in four short acts) 31
Beauty 34
Waiting for You 35
I am not my chair 38
Stuck 41
today it is difficult to write 3
Definition 46
Poseurs 48
The Muse 50
A Little Ado About Nothing 51
Radiance. 53
Why Are We Here? 54

Borders is Closing (A Saturday afternoon; and the passing of a friend.)	56
America 2197	58
Runway 24, Lukla, Nepal (The Attainment of Dreams)	62
The Mode of the Hummingbird	64
Poetic Convergence	67
The Secret to Good Sex	70
Homeland	72
This Morning I Stayed in Bed (for Holley)	75
This Moment in Time	76
Darkness and Light	78
"Take a Drug" (Prelude to the fall of a culture)	80
Love	84
Woman	86
Authenticity	88
Space	89
"God: Getting Bored…"	91
Courtney	94
Farewell on a winter night—I will return	96
Merchants of Small Wars	97
Connecting Dots	100
They Went	102
Love Match	103
Just Because	106
Thanksgiving	108
On Poetry (Art) and Social Responsibility	111
About the Author	119

Michael Graves

Snacking on Bukowski

I go to the bookstore because I'm hungry.
Because I miss the taste of
air that's been slowly seasoned
with thousands of books.

Because I need to sit in a place with a
thousand, thousand doors that open
into the labyrinthine minds
of a thousand, thousand artists.

A place with endless
lines of ink, spilling onto
pages in orderly rows; belying
the wild, raving
luscious canvas within.

A place where staid black and white, blend
to create brighter and more vivid
colors than those that see
the light of day.

Because I need to run my fingers
slowly
down soft
spines
of beautiful stories, wishing
I had time to do them all. My imagination
snacking on candy.

I wander.
I breathe.
I breathe.
My insides relax.

Reflections on a Crystal Wind

I feel the texture of paper
slick as the ice in Spring
or formed from tiny chunks of trees
otherwise left forgotten.

I crack open Bukowski and read the short, broken
lines, slipping down
the textured page.
Just a snack.
(He's always there.)
Until I realize I have to go.
Realize that I've been
smiling the entire time.
And Charles has reminded me
how much I like to read.

  —Graves 12/30/14

Michael Graves

The View from the Lighthouse

I have seen the storms
far-off and approaching.
I have watched the crashing waves
yet to come
run their course.
I have heard the howling wind
in the dark, wet night.

I have watched the tides.

I see the rocks that lie in wait
beneath the shiny surface
of the calm sea.
I see the slow
unstoppable
swell
of the tsunami
seeking
to subsume
the shoreline.

The sea itself is made of changes. Always
changes.

Some, sudden and violent.
Some, transient and fleeting.
Some, deadly and permanent.

With perspective
you learn the difference.

Vicissitudes can kill you.
Even the word sounds like
choppy water.

Life can turn on a dime.
Let it.

Reflections on a Crystal Wind

Allow it to turn, and then
ride it
in your direction.

Anything else, and you founder
or become at last becalmed.

With perspective
you learn the difference.

Just because the water is choppy
does not mean
disaster is certain.
Adrift is not death.
It is simply

adrift.

Know the stable point of land.
Know the star that does not fail.
Know very well, the decision
that means more to you
than life.

And on that, plot your course.
And never

waver.

Do not panic
when the wind hits a fresh gale
when the waters turn angry
and the masts begin to creak and strain.
That is simply the way
of the sea.

Michael Graves

Sailing is at its most exhilarating
when the sails are full
and pulses pound. Provided
you stay the course
and ride out the storm.

Don't change direction, based
on a single stretch of
heavy weather.
If what you seek
was near at hand
you would not be sailing.

      —Graves 8/26/11

Decision

The dream does not exist, that
has not in its conception come
coupled with challenge
as its birth-twin.

Alike, no wish exists
that in its forming thought is void
of gauntlet thrown
to make it so.

Life concatenates
challenge to challenge.
That's what makes it
Life.

To wake and dress. Or to drink
hot coffee
without spilling.

To ascend
the ice-covered
vertical rock face
in a live, raging
gale. Or to fall

into hopeless
riotous love, never
to be the same. Ever.

Life flows.
It does not stop.
That is what makes it
Life.

Michael Graves

The path was void before you came
win or lose.
You decide which fork to walk
and you alone.

Who refuses this is soaked too deep
in need to blame. His head
too thickly bound in batting
to hear the holy songs.

You
and you alone decide:
poison or
life.

The dream does not exist, that
has not in its conception come
coupled with challenge as its birth-twin.

Delight or
poison.
You decide.

—Graves 12/24/10

Steinbeck's Ghost

Steinbeck walks the
short, straight streets along
the weather-worn, wooden walls of Cannery Row
swapping jokes with Ed Ricketts, each
out-shouting the bashing, booming waves. Laughing
like two men sharing the last drink
before the bottle breaks
into flying, sparkling splinters
on the rocks that edge the bay.

Back-slapping they wander
planning the trip to British Columbia to
write "The Outer Shores."
Ed, living for tidepool discoveries
on the gray, windy edge of
Monterey Bay.
John pinching Carol.
Pounding out
psalms of the displaced. Etching
the glass of humanity with
hard lines from a bindlestiff's memory.
Cutting glass with an
Hermes Baby portable typewriter
in the foggy, fecund air of
the Pajaro Valley. Carving
his way into the consciousness
of America with
diamond-hard tales of the wandering underclass.

The wanderlust of the starving is less
lust than hunger and the need
to keep moving. For
to stop is to court the stillness
of death. To face the fear of the fatality of roots
that tie the wandering soul to the earth and
frame the grave which awaits the stationary man.

Michael Graves

Even now, he pounds
in the noisy stillness
amid the roar of gray, autumn waves.
Cutting glass with an
Hermes Baby portable typewriter
in the foggy, fecund air of
the Pajaro Valley.
Dead for forty years.

    —Graves 1/1/15

Beatitudes

Blessed are those who refuse to fail.
For they shall attain
impossible heights.

Blessed is the child who rides out life
alone, and blooms despite all.
For his is the resilience
of the unstoppable.

Blessed are those who give advice and do not
require that it be followed.
For they will be called friends.

Blessed are those who care enough to change conditions
where others will not.
For their lives, while perhaps more trying
will make the greatest difference.

Blessed are those who right the scales.
For their gift to the world
is sanity.

Blessed are those who follow Jerry Garcia and the boys.
For they shall be called Deadheads*
Wait... what?

Blessed are those who acknowledge and forgive the past.
For they will have the clearest
view of the future.

Blessed are those who grace the world with
new viewpoints, new
games and new vistas.
For theirs is the crown of creation.
And they will be the suppliers of dreams.

Michael Graves

Blessed are those willing to honestly help
without hidden agenda.
For they will ease the burden.

Blessed are the defenders and healers of souls.
For they guard the route
to eternity.

Blessed are those who understand the power of responsibility
and the fruitlessness of revenge.
For theirs will be the sanest perspective.

Blessed are those who strive to travel beyond the edge
of what is known.
For theirs is the uncharted realm.

Blessed are those who understand, and move forward
even under the most daunting conditions.
For they will forge the forward path.

And blessed are those who come back.
For some will call them angels.
And they will save
the world.

       —Graves 1/28/11

*"Deadheads" is a term which was affectionately given to fans of the rock band "The Grateful Dead," which achieved iconic status in the 1970's. Jerry Garcia was the band's leader.

Tonight

Tonight, the dead will remain dead.
And we, my love
aloft with life, shall reign
vibrant and shining, while
breath remains within us.
Glowing like two coals born of
incipient fire, bathed in recombinant light.
Memories of another time
sent to a place away, and told
to be still.
For tonight, the dead will remain dead.

    —Graves 6/7/14

Michael Graves

Like Hemingway On The Streets Of Spain

The road stretches long and empty
when the Muse leaves.

The heart aches to capacity, and then overflows
with emptiness.
The wooden palette lays
against the wall, stained
with faded pigment:
A brittle, hollow gourd, once filled with unending
rapacious inspiration and promises

of a future where
creation is as effortless as the sparking
of two ideas moving together in the wet, sultry night.

Water is not coming.
There is no quenching the thirst at
the death of the soul.

I sit and remember times
when life was much like
Hemingway on the streets of Spain. Walking
the cobblestones of Pamplona, already working
on "Death in the Afternoon."

The pulse of life pounding. Coursing with
the weight and texture of that which falls
with night and rises with the streaming
bleeding color of the new day.
And which finally ends
when she leaves
for the last time.

Now, at the end, the winds
of the Pyrenees scrub
the air of Pamplona clean
of the foul smell of blood.

Reflections on a Crystal Wind

The roar of the crowd has gone home, and
the bloodlust (having served its purpose) is politely
folded and placed back into pockets and
purses, like some used, dirty handkerchief to be taken
home and laundered clean in private.
To be reborn in a pristine state.
As though this could hide its nature.

The carcasses of the fallen
have been hauled away
leaving only drag-marks in the dirt; baking
in the languid afternoon.

The matador, so proud of his cheap rhinestones
hums a small tune of the bullfight
tightens his borrowed mask, and
leans back on a thin, unsteady, green chair
in the shadow of the crowded cafe.
He tunes his small guitar sharp from flat.
Waiting for the attention he considers
his due; now that the "noble"
slaughter is over.

The hands of beggars in the
red-dirt road that leads elsewhere, are
lined from overwork
clutching at the air
hoping to get her attention
in the end, fatally
unaware that
the only way
to attract the Muse
is to continue to create.

   —Graves 12/30/14

Michael Graves

"And why," she asked haughtily, "should I say 'You bastards' instead of 'You sons of bitches?'"

On the Use of the Phrase "You Bastards!"

"Sons of bitches" seems so imprecise
neither biting, impactful, it's just not concise.
When delivering a blow
you just want to know
the recipient's paid some kind of price!

"Sons of bitches" just sounds way too passive.
Not direct, kind of prissy and surely not massive
enough to connect with
convey disrespect with
and frankly it's just not harassive.

"You Bastards!" is nicely contusive
concise, clearly said and abusive
enough to impinge
to make the guy cringe
and its meaning is never elusive.

"You Bastards!" is short, but more elegant
and actually really quite eloquent.
It's nicely concise.
poetically precise
And it always fits right in its element.

"You Bastards!" gives more satisfaction.
It really hits home with impaction.
It's never mistaken
or leaves them unshaken
And generally causes some action.

"You Bastards!" is sonorously rich
(and in plural it just fits the niche.)

For singular, though
the best way to go
is cut loose with "You son of a bitch!"

See?

    —Graves 3/29/09

The River

In my life
I swear, I will know you.

I will know the soft, wet
moss surrounding your delicate
trickling wellhead.

I will know each
of your myriad moods
mirroring the terrain
for hundreds of miles.

And I will know
your boisterous, triumphant entry
to the sea.

I will glide
the length of your
twisting
course
dipping my paddle
again and again

into your cool
liquid current
as I pilot my boat
between your smooth
slippery banks
to find your hidden
eddy and quiet ripples.

I will ride your wild
bucking rapids until
spent at last
with heaving chest
weak from exertion
I emerge triumphant, drenched
from your wet embrace.

Reflections on a Crystal Wind

I will race your twisting
length, flying wildly
before your current
like a leaf in a storm.

I will chase the reflection
of the running moonlight
along your banks
in the cool spring night
beneath sparkling stars.

And I will know you, again
and again, until finally

you carry me
home.

—Graves 1/15/14

Michael Graves

The Sea

She is the sea.

Lounging languidly
beneath the hot, azure sky
recumbent and shiny.

Not a care.

Across a tan stretch of sand
soft and wet
she pulls me deep into her
sensuous, undulating waves.

She is the sea.

Her tides: high, low, rip, ebb, stand, red, flood, neap...
I will never
know all of her moods.
Nor understand.

But there is no need.

She is the sea.

She rages before
the winds of
change.

Holding to her own rules, bending
to the will of none.

Her tide ebbs, and
she is sharp rocks
barnacles and
slimy green things.

She is the sea.

I sail her
with my small, wooden boat.

Reflections on a Crystal Wind

Its hull dipping
between her
heaving
swells.

Her rocking, wet
slap
slap
slap
against my
wooden hull
leaves my bare
wind-burned skin
soaked
and wanting more.

She claims neither
responsibility nor care
for my attention.

She is the sea.

Capricious and
frisky in
white-caps, she sparkles
shimmering, wet, moongleam
in the night.
Awaiting my return.
Feigning disinterest, yet
waiting
to be
engaged.

And She is the sea.

—Graves 8/27/14

The Air

You are oxygen to my flame.
Without you, I do not burn.

In your absence
though the night carries no concealing clouds
there is no light.

You are the riotous wind
that stokes the ocean to a frenzied rage.

The breath that silently forms
ripples on the mirrored pond.

You are the air that slides across
my skin in the sultry
wet night.
Lighting fire.

Without you I do not breathe.

   —Graves 5/25/13

Vengeance 'lex talionis' (For the suicide bombers)

The path of vengeance is paved
in blind, smoldering hatred.

Lined with souls already damned, set
one against the other to fall like dominoes.
It does not end
until all lie writhing in the dust.

A hot, dry wind is all that remains
at the end of this path.
A wind which carries no joy
no satisfaction.

"But the law says: 'An eye for an eye!'
It is only just!"

No.
It is not.

"An eye for an eye" is a crime
committed by translators, in thrall to those
thirsting for blood and for self-serving tumult
translating for the convenience of those
who live to wage death.

The proper reading should be:
"For an eye that is taken
an eye should be replaced."

An eye for an eye.

A life for a life is a far
more complex proposition.
It is not true that death, as a solution
is never warranted. But vengeance
begets naught but vengeance.

Michael Graves

A repetition of itself, as a round
in an unholy song, voiced
in an eternally minor chord.
No life. No happiness.

The appearance of satisfaction, real
only to he whose gaze is fixedly inward
who dances alone in his murderous
—"I told you so"—existence.
He is a mote of dust in a barren, soulless
empty land which bears no solace.

You would justify your pain
by adding to the universe, more pain!
You ignorant, self-righteously arrogant child!

You would justify your existence by the death of those
into whose eyes you've never looked!

Justice is a more difficult job.
It is not as easy as killing.
Violence is only done
where fear is first present.

Vengeance begets only death and vengeance.
It does not balance the scale.
But you knew that from the beginning
and did not care; bearing the rage-fueled seed
nurtured only by the compulsion to inflict pain.

If you want true justice:
Get those who created your pain
to understand and face without denying, the
horror of their acts; and then to make
effective and acceptable amends.
By their own choice.
By their own hand.

   —Graves 1/1/15

Taking Off My Watch

Taking off my watch
I was finally naked.

No longer bound by time, and the feeling
that finishing
was urgent.

Trees grow
at their own rate.

Love wraps itself around lives
in its own time.

The Earth moves underneath me
at it's own pacing. Why

should I not do the same?

—Graves 6/28/12

Michael Graves

The Life of Dreams

Dreams don't die.
They just get dropped off somewhere, when
something else with more sparkle comes along.
Or when a soon-to-be former dreamer
decides that "real life" is more important.

REAL LIFE????

What the hell is more important than dreams!?!
"Real life" is a drafty phone booth in a rainstorm
in October, on a concrete sidewalk in a
bad part of town, compared to dreams!

You lose your dreams
and you might as well kill yourself right now.
(Or get some more dreams) because
your life is going to be pointless without them.

"Oh, but I have no more dreams... (*sob*)
they have all been taken from me by
a hard, hard life..."

"Dreaming's so difficult..."

whine

whine

whine.

Do you KNOW how hard it is to make new dreams?

It's the third easiest thing in the universe to do
after being alive; and looking (which is
the second easiest thing.)

If you want dreams, stop resisting them.
Make some!
It's not difficult.

Reflections on a Crystal Wind

And if you get tired of one
get rid of it and create a hundred more!

It's EASY! Unless for some reason, you've decided
that it's more fun to live in that damned phone booth
whining about how no one's provided you any dreams.
Waiting like some metaphysical socialist
for someone to give you the dreams
that they've taken from someone else, simply because
you're too wrapped around your own shortcomings
to come up with a few yourself.

Do you know how EASY it is
to come up with a new dream!?!

Watch.

Think of something that you've always wanted to do.
Now, imagine yourself doing it.

Really. Imagine yourself doing it.
Now, get how good it will feel when you
finally accomplish it.

Steep in that feeling for a minute, and then
take a deep breath and own that feeling.

THAT'S ALL THERE IS TO IT!!!!!

Now, make a thousand more.
Or only three.
And if you get tired of one
or a hundred
get rid of it and make a hundred more!
No one's stopping you.
Except yourself!

"Dreaming's difficult..." Oh, please!

    —Graves 1/1/15

Michael Graves

Friendship

Your enemy is not:

Christian
Muslim
Jewish
Hindu
Buddhist
Shinto
Sikh

He is not:

Palestinian
Israeli
American
Russian
Chinese
Japanese
Iranian
Indian
Pakistani

There are differences between men.
That makes them interesting.
That gives them something to talk about.

Your enemy is the specific man
who would use these differences
to breed distrust, and then
carefully
fan that distrust into hatred.

That man plants seeds that
he has carefully gathered from his own
hatred.
He is a man who knows
no peace except death.

Reflections on a Crystal Wind

For him, there is no sunny laughter of children; only
the sound of young recruits to his cause.
And his cause is death.

He dances like the matador, inflaming
the bull with deception and pain
to the point that it cannot think.
It charges anything that moves.
He leads it to death. Nothing more.

He knows that there is no gain
at the end of his road.

There are differences between men.
That is what makes them interesting.
They share similar dreams.

This man dreams of
setting them at each others throats. He
is enemy to them all.

Children play in green fields
in the warm afternoon.
He watches from the tree-line, hidden
among the weeds. Plotting
ways to turn them into creatures
of hate.

Every country
every religion
every race
has these men.

The war is: All
of us, against the few
of them.

All of us.

    —Graves 9/19/12

Michael Graves

Mountaineer (to Jaxon)

The clouds finally part.

And I see you
in the distance
on the mountain above me, waving.
Like some intransigent diamond
set amongst
the rocks of time.

For you have chosen
the vertical trek
where life is win or die.
The holy light of purpose shines
from your eyes, brighter
than the fiercest star, as you climb.

On a course so few have seen
as yet, or even dared
to imagine, you
industriously plot your way beyond
the line of human sight.

Focused on the rocks above.
Seeking out the next vantage point
from which to reach
a place
closer to your own
eternal sky.

You will reach bounds beyond
any to which I hope to aspire
just now
my son.

And someday (I know) you
will find a way to sink a piton
into clouds
and just keep climbing;

where others would have
long since sought
the descending trail.

It's true, I take another path.
A chimney in between the rocks
while you hammer
piton after
piton into
the living rock
of the mountain
and continue to
ascend its unforgiving, icy
face.

No man resembles my dreams
so much as you, my son.
And somewhere
up the mountain, we will sit
out of the wind
around a fire.
Anchored for a time
to rocks of our own creation.
And share stories of the climb.

   —Graves 1/23/15

Dreams—(in four short acts)

Act I:

Your dreams are
your path

from tragedy
to
joy.

You
decide
to walk the path
or not.

Staying home, with dying dreams
though warm and safe

is tragic.

Act II:

You have never dreamed that
which you cannot
achieve.

And you never will.

This fact
terrifies
some who dream

into disbelief.

It terrifies far more
those who fear

dreamers.

This truth is
as simple

and real

as dust motes
riding sunbeams.

Act III:

Fears:

you create them
you permit them
You adopt them
You own them
You enshrine them
You worship them.

And that is the

only

reason
that they do not
leave.

It is only your fears
that will stop your dreams.

This has always been
a comfort
to the courageous

and to those who suddenly realize that
they are about
to become

courageous.

Act IV:

Joy is in
your right hand
tragedy
in your left.

Both are already in
your grasp.

—Graves 4/30/10

Beauty

Beauty is that of which
when you encounter it
you must drink deeply.

There is no escaping this.

Your eyes draw me in like this.

The delicate folds of the iris in bloom
diaphanous petal balancing a bead
of dew in the morning sunlight
refracting the colors of both.

The hawk riding thermals
motionless yet moving.
Gazing out from height
to the ends of the Earth.
Eyes that miss nothing.

I look away, then look back
to drink more deeply.
Then look away.

When I look back there is
always more.

Your eyes draw me in
like this.

—Graves 1/1/15

Michael Graves

Waiting for You

The flow of time is soft
and silent.

It permeates and
moves. And
does not
stop.

Our sun
at last
softly set
once again.

The spaces between us
filled with darkness.
Until I could no longer
see.

I held your face in my hands. While
the cold night moved
between us, and jealous
in its absence of light
stole yours.

My lungs filled to their brim
with pain
and I sat
alone, watching you. Imagining
your chest moving
with the breath
that never came.

Finally, my lungs emptied
of sound.

Earlier that morning, I had wet a cloth and
carefully cleaned your face.

Reflections on a Crystal Wind

Not because I had to
but because I
still could.

You spoke to me then
in whispers
of flowers
and of the coming
spring, which
would brighten the woods

and promised

we would again walk the hills
and name the small birds
by their song.

I know that in quiet times
we spoke of the fact that
there is no one living
who has not met another
that they are

certain

they have known
before.

Not a single soul.

But this leap—despite
the number of times I know
that I've leapt -
always
seems to be
one of faith.

You and I have danced
this dance
before.

Michael Graves

So many times.
From its joyous resume
to its painful end.

This, to me
is as real as the daffodil
in my hand.

I sit now alone, and
wait. Remembering that
it is only
time.

I am waiting for our next walk
in the clean spring air.

The small birds
are waiting.

   —Graves 10/5/12

I am not my chair

I am not the stories
I tell.

I am not the songs
I sing.

I am not the poetry
I write.

I dream
but I
am not my dreams.

I believe
but I
am not my beliefs.

I think
but I
am not my thoughts.

I am not my accomplishments.
They will stand
without me

I am not my history.
It is a trail,
behind me.

I am not my hands.
They are useless
without me.

I am neither the uniform I wear
nor the
causes
for which I fight.

Michael Graves

I am neither the car I drive
nor the king
I serve.

I am neither my bones
nor the meat package
in my skull.

The problem with fitting
everything
into the framework of what is
already known, is
that nothing new
is ever
discovered.

Supreme conceit:
"The Earth
is the center of
the universe."

"Blood flows through
the body because
of tides."

"Man will never
fly."

I learn from my mistakes.
But I am not
those mistakes.

What I have been taught
has changed me
but I am not
those teachings.

I am eternal
and I
do not age.

I am not
my chair.

    —Graves 9/16/11

Michael Graves

Stuck

The will to do is the child of decision.

Absent decision, and you remain rooted in the half-light.
Neither in darkness nor brilliance.
Waiting for the sunrise that never breaks.
Waiting for the night shrouded in diamonds, which never falls.
And you will never
move.

What may become; does not.

And dreams
for lack of decision
die.

Decision is easy.
Move your hand.
Simple.

Getting to the point of decision can be difficult
but never so toxic
as to sit and rot for lack of courage.

Decide!
Forward or back! Either is better than no movement.
For in motionlessness lies death.

Suspend decision and you remain in a holding pattern
circling the airport until death runs you out of fuel
and landing no longer matters.

Decision is the route from transfixed to action
which is traveled in a flash.

All that is required is:
Decide
and Act.

There's the dime
you're on it.
GET OFF OF IT!

      —Graves 1/1/15

Notes:
"Get off the dime!" An American idiom, meaning: to get started in some action; usually after a period of indecision or inaction. Originally, "get off the dime" was a term used by floor managers in 1920's dance halls, telling dancers to stop standing around and start dancing. Ten cents (a dime) was the cost of a dance. By 1926 the phrase had been extended to other activities. "Quit standing around, and get off the dime!"

Michael Graves

today it is difficult to write

Today sits poised on the brink of
something that I can't
quite

see.

Time fidgets

a snowman trying to melt
in preparation for the coming of summer
on a wintry, mid-December night.

Everything seems just out
of reach.

The idea of writing is fused with boredom
and anticipation throughout.
An unfocused wondering, about
which way to turn.

Rivers of words are glaciers
in the black, arctic night. Frozen
with dissatisfaction more than
anything.

Writing is simple.
It begins with decision.
Writing is a clean, crisp
crafting, of carvings.
Writing is simple.

Though, sometimes blocked
by "What for?"

Today is languid.
Life lingers on the street outside
and negotiates continuance with
any passing traffic willing to listen.

Reflections on a Crystal Wind

I can hear it
through my open window.

I am teetering here
on the edge
of Summer and Winter
trying not to fall
into a cotton-batting void
where no fire sparks the imagination with
the adrenaline spike that
I need, to vault into the next
tight, hot, wet, sweaty project.

To see with passion-glazed eyes
bright with painful creation.
Speeding down the mountain
through sweet, thieving air.
Racing the road ahead
past blurred, huge trees any of which
would dish out death as a favor
while looking, conveniently
the other way.

Speeding into the hot night
beneath the flapping wings of the tiny
erratic bat, who flies with crystal vision
born of a blindness
which is only apparent.

Seek not to be remembered for what
you have done. Seek instead
to ride forward on the ramifications of
your accomplishments.
For you will be back to ride
those rippling waves to shore.

No one
is eternal.

Michael Graves

All are eternal, and in the
stone night none really sleep.
Dying is just a ruse to
confound spirits too bored to see
the repeating game.

I bathe in molten lava, cool to the touch
drenched in the passion of carving
out a universe in the pixels
of my touchstone to God
and the denizens who dwell
beyond the bounds of time
out beyond the click of the
clock—knowing that the ravages of time
are only a masquerade
that we play to sample the lower emotions
that are—in our natural state—difficult to reach
because: Why should we?

The spirit flies, not needing to—being everywhere at once
and locating by choice only.
The rush, a contrived boost to the dismissal
of boredom from
the walls
of the castle, where I sit
thinking
about
things.

Because today
it is difficult to write.

      —Graves 1/1/15

Definition

It's not who you claim to be that counts.
The surface of the lake mirrors the sky.
Nothing more.
It holds no clouds. No sun.
Only borrowed reflection.

No transgression escapes
without consequence.
And omission, though unfelt at first like
a razor, cuts deepest.

The warm, willing love
left behind.
The gift, selected with care
and never delivered.
The act of kindness
delayed until too late.
The wrong, witnessed
and left unopposed.

Your actions define you.
Nothing else.

The unwritten is never seen.
The unspoken, never heard.

Your actions form the poetry
or the cliche
that is your life.

Sonnet
Novel
Epithet
Graffiti.

Edit.

Michael Graves

Or not.

It's your life.

>   —Graves 11/15/15

Poseurs

In thrall to the god of Baseless Awe, they glitter.
Not radiant. Rather, an imitation of radiance.
Theft by reflection.
Tinsel without depth.

The attention of those who know no better
than to senselessly dart at the light, their
ultimate reward. Not admiration.
For that would require accomplishment.

All is for show.

Adorned like minor Emperors, they
strut. Naked in carefully tailored garb
stitched with threads of
folly, dyed in hues of
pretentious affectation.

They pretend—and they believe that this
is the same as accomplishment.
That the paraded pretense of pride is sufficient.
Poseurs, with no further goal than
to appear in the light as genuine.
For long enough to impress.
For long enough to cash in.
And that is all.

To appear as—rather than to be.

It has come then, to this:
The apparency of importance, now
has the capacity to hold sway.
Appearance alone, sufficient to evoke respect
requiring no proof of capability—of value.
Just noise and pretense.

Michael Graves

This is the behavior of hollow sheep
fearful of commitment.
The wolves leer.
    —Graves 12/25/15

The Muse

She respects no schedule
save her own. And that

is the first thing one must learn
very, very well.

In her company
I have felt the light bending
through the cells of the inner veins of the crocus
unfolding slowly in sunlight and dew.

I have heard the moonlight singing
like a thousand haunted violins
as it slid coarsely across a thousand blades of frosted grass
in the winter night.

From her I have learned
that what appears to be
is more often than not:
not.

And that which is only imagined
has existed forever.

My wife has no concerns for where I go.
She knows that if she looks and cannot find me
I will be in the tent of the Muse.

   —Graves 10/21/15

Michael Graves

A Little Ado About Nothing

Today, I wrote a poem about something
that left out nothing.

And since nothing was left out
it feels a little lacking
because it's all about nothing.

I'm wondering now whether or not
I should have added nothing more
about nothing
or added something more
about nothing.

It's difficult to say.
Because nothing, being a somewhat slippery thing
is hard sometimes to grasp.
After all, nothing... is nothing.

On the other hand:

When you do nothing
you're really doing something
by doing nothing.
And then again, when you do something
you're not doing nothing.
Unless that something is really
nothing at all.
In which case, it's nothing.

Nothing, after all, is important.
If there was no nothing
how could you walk in-between something
and something?

How could you separate this and that
if there was not nothing
between them?

So, nothing is not without consequence.
Look all you want, and you can't spot nothing.
Because clearly nothing's there.
So actually, you can. But only if you realize you're
seeing nothing, and that there is
truly nothing to see.

As I said: Today, I wrote a poem about something
that left out nothing.
This bothered me a bit, because
the subject was also nothing.
A balancing act over nothing? Perhaps.
It's possible, though, that I'm simply being
overly concerned about nothing.

      —Graves 7/31/15

Radiance

In the beginning, it seems just
a bright
light.

Most stars are

content to twinkle
to politely sparkle
in the cool night sky.

Born sparkling
that is all
the more to which they
attain.

Other stars
pierce the darkness with
such

fierce
radiance

that the world is changed.

Brilliance is a natural
quality. Radiance, (as you know)

takes work.

But in radiance
lies the capacity, to reach
into the darkness, and

to change the world.

   —Graves 8/7/11

Why Are We Here?

A friend of mine once said to me
that he wasn't really clear,
on the reason behind existence,
on the answer to: "Why are we here?"

Are we here to forge a cleaner soul,
to take our turn at bat?
To wrap ourselves around a pole,
and learn new things from that?

Are we here to learn great truths
and tip the scales to balance true?
Are we here to keep the game in play,
to give Karma something to do?

Are we here to find the perfect match
of fortune and true love?
And to find out after searching,
that they rarely go hand in glove?

Are we here to cook the perfect batch
of some outrageous dish?
Or grant a dying child the right
to have his perfect wish?

Are we here to solve deep mysteries
that make the world go 'round?
(If a tree falls in the forest, alone,
does it really make a sound?)

Are we here to differentiate
minutiae from profound?
Or thinking, transubstantiate
our way out of the ground?

And having done so, will it mean much,
as one's life unwinds;
to solve the deepest mysteries,

Michael Graves

to find the greatest finds?
Now I suppose, to some degree,
these things have some import.
And some of these will give one peace,
if only of a sort.

But really, when the course is run
how much of it will matter?
See, one might save the universe, or
be trapped by senseless chatter.

To make a choice between these paths:
Which one will carry true?
Is truthfully the only thing
of value to me and you.

It's not a stupid question, though,
I've given it some thought.
The answer, my friend,
to "Why are we here?"
may simply be: "Why not?"

   —Graves 2/3/12

Reflections on a Crystal Wind

Borders is Closing (A Saturday afternoon; and the passing of a friend.)

I will miss the smell of books.
Bound paper. Ink on a page.
And their coffee.

A place to sit, on Pacific Avenue
out of the rain
and write.

It was my version of
Hemingway's "clean, well-lighted place"
(without the despair, loneliness
or nihilistic taint.)

There is something that feels sacred
about a repository of books

for sale or not.

And Borders was one
of the places where
from time to time
I went to write, to peruse
and to wonder at
the thoughts of others.

Stacks of friends-in-paper
—of like minds
or not.
A place to go, and touch pages.

To stand in the lighted space, and feel
smooth
paper beneath my fingertips.
And feel the words
of others
in my eyes.

Michael Graves

It's not that I mind Amazon
or Kindle or Nook
and the like—and truly
I've shopped the pixel places
but

there is something holy about
"the bookstore"
as an intersection of intellectual
pathways.
A nexus.
A springboard of
dimensional collaboration.

Its occupants were literate.
Thirsty for
words.
Capable of considering
the ideas of another in order to
reach the lofty places—the great open places in
their minds.
Or simply to scratch the itch
of curiosity.

I wonder if the Library at
Alexandria
was like that
before it was sacked.

      —Graves 10/18/14

America 2197

You are not what you once were. Nothing
is.
Life changes. Life
evolves. Life
encompasses. Or life
dies.

Where once you lounged, cloaked
in alabaster privilege. Steel
ribbons stretching edge to
edge, binding
east to west. Sleepless
fires in your massive coal forges spewing
forth your iron might.
You now sing

the tight, electric harmony.
Photons eclipse electrons.
Cloud surmounts earth.
Lines, long ago fallen before
the ubiquitous Net have been carried away
like pruned canes in a
vineyard now out of season.
Your roots have lengthened
and mingled, drawing life from the ends
of the spherical Earth.

You scan the far horizon with
Viking eyes; fiercely blue
fearing nothing.
The cold wind strews your flaming
Scottish hair and you smile
the knowing smile of one
certain to win all.

Michael Graves

On the night air, your sweet Arabian lips call my name
with cool aplomb and draw me close
murmuring tales of the Rub'al-Khali.
Of Dubai, before
the oil came
to your new home.
The sultry breeze whispers against
your smooth skin: Ebony silk
in the quiet morning of this new day. The cruel
uphill fight to attain, attain, attain
now so old as to be
legend. A curio
on a bracelet of charms.

Your voice dances in my ears
my sweet Parvati, and whets
all of my senses.
The gods of ancient Dwarka speak
through your fingers, and weave the future.
The ancient navigators of
Micronesia, now plot courses past
the stars with ease.
The sea was, after all
just practice.

The tango of the Argentine
speaks in your blood, and cries out
for the inevitable conquest.
Your breath quickens at the scent
of opportunity, for you are one
not without the fiercest of passions.
The view from the peaks of Aconcagua and Chimborazo
king and queen of the Andes
has sharpened the acuity of vision
that you bring to your new home
to the point that the hawk—not the eagle—is jealous.
For you too now share the aerie.

You are as unstoppable
as the unkillable
persistence of your
beautiful Russian forebears.
As transcendently enduring in the face
of adversity as the ancient monks
of the Tibetan high plateau. Of
the pilgrim looking toward Mount Kailash,
from Idaho.

You are so much more than you were.
And so much less than you will be.
My love.
My America.

   —Graves 2/12/15

Notes:
Rub'al-Khali: The Rub' al Khali or Empty Quarter is the largest sand desert in the world, encompassing most of the southern third of the Arabian Peninsula. It includes most of Saudi Arabia and areas of Oman, the United Arab Emirates, and Yemen. The desert covers some 250,000 square miles.

Parvati: Parvati, also known as Gauri, is a Hindu goddess, nominally the second consort of Shiva, the Hindu god of destruction and rejuvenation. Generally considered a benevolent goddess, she also has wrathful incarnations such as Durga and Kali. She is the gentle aspect of Mahadevi, the Great Goddess, with all other goddesses being her incarnations or manifestations.

Dwarka: Dwarka is a city and a municipality of Jamnagar district in the Gujarat state in India. Also known as Dwarawati in Sanskrit literature, Dwarka is one of the seven most ancient cities in the country. The legendary city of Dwarka was the dwelling place of Lord Krishna.

Aconcagua: Aconcagua is the highest mountain in the Americas (22,837 feet). It is located in the Andes mountain range, in the province of Mendoza, Argentina. It is one of the Seven Summits.

Chimborazo: Chimborazo is the highest mountain in Ecuador (20,564 ft). While Chimborazo is not the highest mountain by elevation above sea level, its location along the equatorial bulge makes its summit the farthest point on the Earth's surface from the Earth's center.

Mount Kailash: A peak in the Transhimalaya range in Tibet. It is considered a sacred place in four religions: Bön, Buddhism, Hinduism and Jainism. Tibetan Buddhists call it "Kangri Rinpoche" meaning "Precious Snow Mountain". Bon texts give it many names: "Water's Flower", "Mountain of Sea Water", "Nine Stacked Swastika Mountain". For Hindus, it is the home of the mountain god Shiva and a symbol of his power symbol "Om"; for Jains it is where their first leader was enlightened; for Buddhists, it is the navel of the universe; and for adherents of Bon, it is the abode of the sky goddess Sipaimen.

Runway 24, Lukla, Nepal (The Attainment of Dreams)

To reach the summit of Everest
you must land on Runway 24
in Lukla, Nepal.

There is no other way.

It has a cliff at one end.
A mountainside at the other.
It is only
one thousand
five hundred
feet long.

It is the most dangerous runway
in the world.

But it is the gateway
to dreams.

To reach Everest
you must walk the Khumbu Glacier.
But first
you must scale the death trap that is the Khumbu Icefall.

To earn the chance to do either
you must land on Runway 24.
You must commit.

Runway 24 is the step beyond common reality.
Every prior experience
is shared with those who are content
to live on ordinary ground.

The flight from Kathmandu takes 35 minutes.
The weather changes
quickly.

When the opportunity for flight presents itself
you must take it.

Michael Graves

Or remain below.

You must commit.

There is no other way.

The light changes on the summit of Everest
from minute to minute.
No two climbers ever

see exactly the same view
from the height.

As sure as the clouds
of ice crystals rise
on the ragged winds
like a plume
from the summit of Everest

it is there
for the taking.

To attain
you must commit.
You must land on Runway 24.

     — Graves 10/2/15

Note:
The Khumbu Icefall lies at the head of the Khumbu Glacier, on the Nepali slopes of Mount Everest, not far above Base Camp. The icefall is one of the most dangerous stages of the South Col route to Everest's summit. It is estimated that the glacier advances 3 to 4 feet down the mountain every day. Large crevasses open with little warning. The towers of ice found at the icefall have been known to collapse suddenly, sending huge blocks of ice tumbling down the glacier. They can range from the size of cars to the size of 12-story buildings.

This poem is dedicated to those who have landed.—MG

The Mode of the Hummingbird

When you drop it, a stone falls.
It happens.
Your opinion on the matter is not required.

When you blame
your shortcomings on another, you
swear blind fealty to a lie.
You abdicate the dream.
You hand the knife
to the highwayman and lay bare
your throat.
Because this attitude will eventually kill you.

It's harsh.
But it's true.
Like a falling stone.

Those who seek to blind you, or
bend you to their will
will tell you otherwise. It is
their benefit that interests them. Not truth.
If you bend, you become their marionette.
Jeanne d'Arc can cite you
chapter and verse on this.

At the beginning, nothing
is determined.
Your road does not begin
at it's end.
It does not start in a state
of completion.
It leads not yet to failure
nor to success.
That which you seek to achieve
is there before you.
Waiting.

Michael Graves

The hummingbird does not see himself
as small.
He simply sees the world
as large.
And in that mode
he flies.

The limit placed on you
by another
is a lie.
The limit that you place
on yourself
is your chain. It is
the barrier you cannot
surmount.

Unless (of course) you change
your mind.

And when you truly, fully
change your mind
you will find, that removing the barrier
is very much like
taking off a coat on a hot day.

After all

the world is
only large.

   —Graves 12/9/14

Notes:
mode: n. 1. a. A manner, way, or method of doing or acting.

Jeanne d'Arc: (Eng. Joan of Arc) (ca. 1412–May 30, 1431) was born to a peasant family in northeast France. She said that she had received visions from God instructing her to support Charles VII and recover France from English domination late in the Hundred Years' War.

She was sent by the uncrowned King Charles VII to the siege of Orléans as part of a relief mission; and gained prominence after the siege was lifted in only nine days. Several additional swift victories led to Charles VII's coronation at Reims.

On May 23, 1430 Jeanne was captured at Compiegne by the English-allied Burgundian faction. Subsequently, she was put on trial by the pro-English Bishop of Beauvais, Pierre Cauchon on a variety of spurious, politically-motivated charges in an attempt to undermine the legitimacy of the succession of King Charles VII. She was found guilty of heresy and burned at the stake. She was about 19 years old.

Twenty-five years after her execution, an inquisitorial court authorized by Pope Callixtus III examined the trial, pronounced her innocent, and declared her a martyr.

Poetic Convergence

Poetry should not simply be
the act of finding words that rhyme
and placing them in

measured

lines, any more than sex should be
the monotonous, repetitive rubbing
together of skin in the dark.

Words mingle like potential
lovers in festival masks
considering convergence.

Lacking direction, they mill about
forming lame conversation and
desperate small talk
hoping for more. Looking
for meaningful (or not) conjunction.
For counterpoint, wrapping
hungrily one around the other
in penetrating juxtaposition.
Shuddering alliteration.
Yearning for the onomatopoeic concatenation of sounds
which in the end, fill the room, and hang
in the mind.

Words are sounds, rolled back
and forth on the warm
slippery surface of the mind's tongue.
Moved and molded again and again
until ready to be entered
on the page.

The best arrangements are rarely
predictable.

Twist them until they scream
with delight.
Tweak them until their meaning is
rigid and undeniable.
Take them and travel to a place of wonder, because
cliche is so
humdrum-predictable.
The steady rhythm of a dull saw that
puts
you
to sleep.

No life.
No excitement.
No spice. No tightening
gasp of delight
in the mind, at a glimpse of something
hoped for. A door
that opens into a wondrous new place
of transcendent ecstasy. A glimpse
of the holy vision.

When poetry causes the mind to catch
its breath; then
it is working.

   —Graves 11/22/12

Notes:
Counterpoint: The technique of combining two or more melodic lines in such a way that they establish a harmonic relationship while retaining their linear individuality.

Juxtaposition: An act or instance of placing close together or side by side, especially for comparison or contrast.

Alliteration: The repetition of the same sounds, or of the same kinds of sounds at the beginning of words, or in stressed syllables, as in: "she sells sea shells by the seashore" or "oh! oh! oh! oh! Ohhhhh! ohhhhh...". Modern alliteration predominantly involves consonants. Certain literary traditions, such as Old English verse, also alliterate using vowel sounds.

Onomotopoeiatic (from onomotopoeia): The naming of a thing or action by a vocal imitation of the sound associated with it (as buzz, hiss, smack, bang, bash, cuckoo, meow, honk, or boom).

Concatenation: A chain; a sequence of things or sounds related to, or dependent upon each other. Ex. "The concatenation of explosions from the string of firecrackers." Or "Like the concatenation of defensive soundbites following accusation in an election year."

Dull saw: A saw is an old saying or commonly repeated phrase or idea.

The Secret to Good Sex

To seek the grail seems less involved
than the secret to good sex.
Though many seek and seek and seek
and end up as miserable wrecks.
They pen the things that work for them
and end up sounding sappy.
If you want to solve the secret,
simply sleep with someone who's happy.

Sleep with someone miserable,
and you'll end up stained with gloom.
You'll wake in the morning and find
that they simply want you out of the room.
The sex was bad, their life is bad
and you're now the brunt of complaints.
Conveniently, you're near at hand,
though by now you're wishing you ain't.

A train wreck is a joy
compared to sleeping with someone unhappy.
Give it a shot and believe it or not,
your life will be nothing but crappy.
Take this course
and you'll live a life that's laden with regret.
A safer and more joyous game
is classic Russian roulette.

If all you know are happy folks,
it's far less problematic.
Unless, of course, you misconstrue
and they're actually sociopathic.
If you'd care to test my premise
and pursue it to its conclusion,
You'll find that it's an easy one
that results in little confusion.

Michael Graves

The answer then is simple
and your life will be quite snappy.
If you just make the person you're sleeping with
exquisitely, delightfully happy.
    —Graves 12/30/14

Homeland

I live in a land that lies between
Ars Poetica and Daylight.
Near Poesia the sea of dreams
shining softly in the moonlight.

'cross the Isthmus of Illusion, down
the River of Riotous Times.
You'll find me there, beneath a tree
happily batting out rhymes.

Beyond the Plains of Perilous Plight
and the Hills of Recombinant Verse.
It's a land where poetry lingers like clouds
in a sky you'd just love to traverse.

In a huge balloon made of phrases and verbs
tied together with lines of conjunction.
Buoyed by verses so light and so clear
so delightful they near' restrict function.

On the other hand, there's another land
to the east, where the verse is so sodden
that poets (who are normally creatures of light) are
quite proud of being downtrodden.

In Pedantia, poetry's a serious thing
made with scary rules and compunction.
With so many levels of interpretation
you can barely retain mental function.

With references so arcane and obscure
that it's easy to question validity.
Except when you note that the poet who wrote them
died drowning in excess perfidy.

Clarity in poetry's a dangerous thing
that terrifies scholars and hokes
who, failing to see to the bottom of things

bind their words up in mirrors and smoke.
The effortless flow of simplicity, just
evades their awareness, I guess.
And all they intend, at the end of it all
is to wow and confuse and impress.

But the poetry of truth can be simple and clear
without so much as a riddle.
Its premise is such that it needs no device
no artifice nor tremulous fiddl(ing).

A poetic statement, clear and concise
understood by any who read it
is vastly superior to one made with lines
so confusing they act to defeat it.

A piece thickly bound in pedantics
based on overworked pontification
makes a far better sermon, than poetic verse
as it's rooted in obfuscation.

My homeland though, is in a place
where poetry's thankfully brimming
with lightness and grace, laid out at a pace
that doesn't set your head spinning.

I come from a land that lies between
Ars Poetica and Daylight.
Near Poesia, the sea of dreams
shining softly in the moonlight.

'cross the Isthmus of Illusion, down
the River of Riotous Times.
You'll find me here at the end of my days
happily batting out rhymes.

  —Graves 9/22/12

Notes:

Ars Poetica: Ars Poetica is a term meaning "The Art of Poetry" or "On the Nature of Poetry". Early examples of Artes Poeticae by Aristotle and Horace have survived and many other poems bear the same name.

Poesia: Italian/Portuguese: Poetry

Pedantica: A fictional land; from Pedantic: "Characterized by a narrow, often ostentatious concern for book learning and formal rules. Marked by a narrow, often tiresome focus on or display of learning, and especially its trivial aspects."

Hoke: One who hokes or "hokes up". Originally from "hokum", "to hoke", means: "to alter or manipulate so as to give a deceptively or superficially improved quality or value (usually followed by up): as in: "a political speech hoked up with phony statistics."

One who hokes things up, is therefore a "hoke."

Michael Graves

This Morning I Stayed in Bed (for Holley)

This morning I stayed in bed
with you.

I kissed your face.
I smelled your hair.

And felt your warmth
in a way that
I had not
before.

This morning I stayed.
And a different future opened.
And my eyes opened.
And I saw a place that
I had never been.

Promises to others
I left strewn across the bedroom floor
to pick up
at another time.

This morning I stayed.
And watched you breathe.
And with each breath
the outside world felt farther
and further away.

We watched the leaves.
We fed the cat.
And every little
thing
was right.

Because this morning I stayed
with you.

—Graves 2/13/15

This Moment in Time

You determine this moment in time
no one else.

Its creation is yours.
You conceive it.
You shape it.
You give it life.

Yield the creation of this moment to another, and
you suspend yourself
in air
above a chasm
hanging (or not) at their choice.
Your life no longer your own.

Fame, approval, permission granted
by another, may be
taken away.

Except by your own decision
what you create, cannot.

Yield your will to create
and your forward path becomes chosen
at the whim of another.
The journey bereft of the
joyfulness born of creation.

You create your life
and include others (or not).
You create your future
and include others (or not).

Recall a time when you were truly happy.
Recall a time that you loved someone deeply.
Recall a time when things were joyfully real.
Recall a time when you succeeded.
Recall a time when you won.

Michael Graves

These things will be with you, always.
Regardless of what follows.

The creation of joy, of purpose
is within you. It is a gift that you give
yourself.

It is a gift that you share with others, or not.

Build your own life. Create your own dreams.
Live true to your own goals.
Speak your own truths.

None of these can be taken from you.
Unless you first elect it so.

   —Graves 4/4/15

Darkness and Light

First there is darkness.
Until there is light.

Light is not the natural way of things. It is
created. Absent light
the universe is dark.

There is first absence
until you approach.
I feel your warm breath on my neck.
Your presence (as it always does) changes
the essence of my experience. Much

in the way that there is
first cold. Until it is
replaced with heat.

There is inaction before action
status quo before change
stillness before motion.

Prior to hatred there is
the willingness to understand.

We attract that which we fear
because we work to push it away.
In pushing, we must make contact.
And in contacting, we draw it near.

Create, instead, in the direction in
which you would travel.
And the things you fear will
drop away behind you. They cannot
keep up without your help.

The reason that we do not achieve, has nothing
to do with anyone else.

Michael Graves

Life is as we perceive it and
as we empower it. Prior
to perception, it is not our life.

    —Graves 4/11/15

"Take a Drug" (Prelude to the fall of a culture)

Wearing a frown?
Take a drug.
Can't keep it down?
Take a drug.
Head hurts?
Take a drug.
Energy in spurts?
Take a drug.
Too much energy?
Take a drug.
Want more synergy?
Take a drug.
Feeling too happy?
Take a drug.
Feeling sappy?
Take a drug.
Too contentious?
Take a drug.
Feeling licentious?
Take a drug.
Can't get to sleep?
Take a drug.
Thinking too deep?
Take a drug.
Feeling tired?
Take a drug
Feeling wired?
Take a drug.
Kids bugging you?
Give 'em drugs;
won't study in school?
Give 'em drugs.
Can't get wet?
Take a drug.
Lost a bet?

Michael Graves

Take a drug.
Feeling nervous?
Take a drug.
Can't get service?
Take a drug.
Can't stay dry?
Take a drug.
Wanna get high?
Take a drug.
Feeling antsy?
Take a drug.
Not enough fantasy?
Take a drug.
Can't stay sober?
Take a drug.
Feeling hungover?
Take a drug.
Can't stop talking?
Take a drug.
Problems walking?
Take a drug.
Can't get it up?
Take a drug.
Still can't schtupp?
Take a drug.
Can't talk to people?
Take a drug.
Feeling too anal?
Take a drug.
Nose feels itchy?
Take a drug.
Feeling bitchy?
Take a drug.
Peeing too much?
Take a drug.
Losing touch?
Take a drug.

Reflections on a Crystal Wind

Cannot pee?
Take a drug.
Feel too free?
Take a drug.
Got an erection lasting more than four hours?
Call a hooker. (Wait. What?...)
Take a drug.
Scared of heights?
Take a drug.
Can't sleep nights?
Take a drug.
Can't lose weight?
Take a drug.
Can't get a date?
Take a drug.
Feeling too skinny?
Take a drug.
Think you're a ninny?
Take a drug.
All worked up?
Take a drug.
Want to blow things up?
Take a drug.
Got a cough?
Take a drug.
Can't get off?
Take a drug.
Feeling too calm?
Take a drug.
Don't want to be a mom?
Take a drug.
Can't eat food?
Take a drug.
Gotta get nude?
Take a drug.
Eating too much?
Take a drug.

Michael Graves

Out of touch?
Take a drug.
Feeling snappy?
Take a drug.
Too damn happy?
Take a drug.

It's a wonder we don't rattle when we dance.
For that matter, it's a wonder that we dance at all.

    —Graves 5/8/14

Notes:
Schtupp: To engage in coitus.

Love

Before it all began.
Before all of this.
Before I touched you with my eyes and
felt the quick, indrawn breath.
Before we rode the kaleidoscope—the
slippery gamut of textures.
Before I heard you call my name
in the night.
Before the dark sky wrapped itself
in moonlight, in protest against
the uninvited dawn.
Before it all began.
I knew that I knew you.

In the gentle movement of the night air
beyond the mountain, the crow
rides the winds
in search of shelter.
In the night, thinking of home
I hear you sigh.
I feel your breath
warm and moist
on my neck.

In the secret places
where pools join and
overflow their banks, the otter dives
beneath the surface. You shudder
and make delightful sounds.

I know now, that it is possible
to reach without arms of blood and bone.
I know your thoughts before you speak.
It seems the moon always crosses the sky
—blatantly, or in hiding. Either way
I can feel you.

Michael Graves

Between such as us
there is no distance.

If I must wait a thousand years
for our paths to cross again
I will know you.

    —Graves 2/13/15

Woman

Too often man lives doomed. In love
with beauty alone. An image
woven in sensation, expectation and
delight. Composed of equal parts: vibrant thoughts and
immortal expectations. Like
some wondrous, conjured creature sprung
full-grown from sorcerer's brew:
A dash of impossible
a pinch of unattainable, simmered
in unimaginable beauty
brought forth before the shining moon
to wander Earth for him alone.

Bereft, he lives
unable to paint into reality
the portrait, large enough to
encompass the scope of his imaginings. Never
realizing that the sweeping size
of his expectations
is far
too
small

and far
too
over-thought
to fit
the truth which
awaits him
should he but see
what is there
and
what is not
and
in comprehension, begin
by saying, simply "Hello".

Michael Graves

The only hope that he has
is to not die before
realizing that worlds beyond splendor are his
for the taking, should only
he grasp
this single concept.

      —Graves 10/3/14

Authenticity

No one ever won by believing
in the virtue of tremulous whispers.
By stooping gratefully
before the dripping axe of a scornful king.

Everything that you do etches your presence on the future.
Don't allow your message to be blunted by mice
watching fearfully from the sidelines, wringing their hands.
Or perverted by those cloaked in shadows, leering
as you dance to their terrible music.

Don't do it as "someone else" would do it.
Don't write as you "think a writer should;"
or paint as you "think a painter would;"
or design in fearful conformity to "the rules."

Do things as you would do them with no one to answer to.
Anything else is to live a life of shallow deaths
waiting cautiously for the deep one
which brings your struggling hesitancy to an end.

It's your shot—this life.
Do it right.

—Graves 5/29/15

Michael Graves

Space

You live your life in the space that you create.
Nobody else owns it.
Nothing else controls it.
It is yours. It exists
in tandem with the space
of others.
But it is yours.

You are free to move
or not.
Nothing stands in your way, unless
you elect it so.
(And then it's usually
for some entertainment purpose. One
of the many hazards of being
bored.)

It is as high
as wide
as broad
as deep
as light
as dark
as rife with danger or with
sparkling opportunity
as you make it.

And you make it
simply by deciding that it is there.
Before that, it was naught.
After that, it is.

(Too easy, right?)
Light or darkness
mass or absence
matter not.

Reflections on a Crystal Wind

Up to you.
No one can interfere with it
unless you allow it. Which
you might, from time to time
and perhaps forget that you have
just for the entertainment value of this.

The: "What!?!? How the hell!!!?..."
of it.
Entertainment. See?
But it is still your space.
And it interacts with
the space of others only
as you decide.

You don't have to believe it.
That's entertainment, too.
Your choice.

You create your life
in your own space.
Nobody owns it.
Nothing controls it
Except you.

And in your own space
nothing stands
in your way.

—Graves 2/6/15

"God: Getting Bored..."

"I've watched over you
since before you crawled
in the dirt.

Babysitting
after long enough
becomes tedious.

I catch myself thinking that
this
should not be the full-time occupation
of an immortal, sentient being.

I love you

but

I am getting tired of
always having to

follow

the

money

like dirty footprints

across the kitchen floor
to find out what
you're up to.

You buy guns
when you should be
learning.

You breed diseases for killing
when you should be
helping the hungry child.

Reflections on a Crystal Wind

You choke the air, when
you should be playing.

You poison the seas, when
you should be saving
your future.

You are old enough, now
to wage
the final
war.

There are few—
too few —

who shine brightly enough to
make my job
interesting, at all.

I am

this!

close!

to kicking you

out of the house!

And if you don't survive... well
there are other
canvases to paint.

There are other places
to populate with flowers
and sentience.

I am not your excuse to kill.
I am not your reason to suppress.
I am not your justification for hatred.
I am not your excuse for theft.
I am not your right to wreak havoc.

Michael Graves

It

does

not

MATTER! which
of my names
you invoke.

I am getting TIRED of
babysitting.

Despite what you think
my patience is NOT eternal. And
saying that it is
does NOT!
make it so.

Carelessly electing me
to clean up
your mess

leaving it to me
to pull your disingenuous hand
back from the fire
yet again
will no longer do.

Maybe now is the time
to say
'Fix it yourself.'

You need to clean up your room."

      —Graves 12/5/15

Courtney

If way exists
to get it done
she will.

Little did I realize
(at first)
my youngest
had cut a deal
with the universe
and it lost.

Yet, she finds snails
and squirrels
delightful company.
Go figure.

The secret (and benevolent)
Queen of the Universe
talks to snails.

And for all I know,
they talk back.

Do you need a building
built from nothing, in Italy?
A galaxy strung with stars?
Old news...
already done.
(Yes, really...)

And why do I sense
that was just
for practice?

Her effortless intention
could burn holes
in the sun.

Michael Graves

(For my sake I hope
she doesn't take THAT
on as a project
on some cloudy afternoon.)

How could I live without
this sprite.
This effortlessly competent
hero.
This player
of vast games.

Rushing the barricades!
("What barricades?" she says...)

How she does this
I have yet to fathom.
I guess
there are
no
barriers
at the edges
of her personal
universe.

      —Graves 5/21/10

Farewell on a winter night—I will return

My clock is ticking, tightly wound, behind its placid dial.
It walks where once it ran, and speaks of things I've left undone.
And though it makes you sad, I'm only leaving for a while.

The night is dark, and in its depth, appearances beguile,
yet darkness, though it hides the view, will bring the rising sun.
My clock, is ticking, tightly wound behind its placid dial.

Your reddened eyes show disbelief, and joy has left your smile;
yet each of us will bid farewell once earthly course is run.
And though it makes you sad, I'm only leaving for a while.

So much is left to do, I've yet to span so many miles.
It seems unfair that I should leave what seems has just begun.
My clock, is ticking, tightly wound behind its placid dial.

I'll see you once again, my love, no virtue's in denial
of what we know we've done before and then again, begun.
And though it makes you sad, I'm only leaving for a while.

Persephone will still bless dew-kissed springtime with her smile;
while blinding fools to wonders clearly far beyond their ken.
My clock's still ticking, tightly wound behind its placid dial.
And though it makes you sad, I'm only leaving for a while.

  —Graves 3/29/14

Michael Graves

Merchants of Small Wars

"The first thing we do, let's kill all the lawyers."
(Dick the Butcher, Henry the 6th, Act 4, Scene 2—
William Shakespeare)

The playing finally
stopped.

The last echo
of music died away:
sucked into solid, reliable
well-used walls.

The band packed up its things.
Our dance, which had begun
with such riotous abandon
was finally over.

We parted.
Speaking acquaintances

knowing that there would not be
another dance.

No more summer nights.
Not a good
night kiss left.

And we proceeded to begin
again, to cut
our own separate paths.

Love, long ago had bled out
into now-dried pools
on a stained, kitchen floor.

Reflections on a Crystal Wind

Perhaps we wished then, to leave
some dignity intact
some humanity for things
gone tragically wrong.
Perhaps, not.

In any case, it was not to be
allowed
for waiting at the door
briefs in hand, were the merchants
of small wars.

Vampires of the emotional night.
Condemned by choice to stalk the
dark, decaying side of human existence.
Feeding on the detritus
of dead and rotting love.

Sucking what life-heat remains
from the embers of hatred.
Fanned by their sly, foul breath.

Pandering physicians of
perniciously-strengthened, vengeance.

Setting half against former half.
Completing the cleave
of what once, you said, could never
be broken.

Fanning flames of malice
with surgical precision into a searing hatred
not known in the wars of State.

Seeking not to heal
but to take.

"But we are only establishing agreements
to allow life to continue!"

Michael Graves

"We are the merchants of small wars.
You will divide, and we will prevail.

And settlements will be made..."

    —Graves 1/1/15

Connecting Dots

We live engulfed
by the lower part of the same sky.
All of us.

We breathe pieces of air
which we have shared by proxy
(from time to time)
on a warm Spring day, when the sky held

just

so

many clouds.

We see the crimson afterglow which heralds night
and speaks of things to come. And wonder
what the day has left in store.

We love.

We hold sleeping dreams, until it is time
for them to awaken or
to be set free.

We sleep.

We wake—for sleeping can only go on so long
and move (in one fashion or another)
through the day.

We hunger for that which we do not have
(yearn seems such an affected, small word
in this case)
if only in noting its absence.

We relish that which we realize we have. And lose
at some point, that which we do not.

Lines between dots connect us all.

Michael Graves

Connect us all.

We die.
We wonder about what comes next.

    —Graves 1/1/15

Notes:
In activity books for children there are often pictures which are formed by connecting the dots with a line. Connecting the dots forms the picture. As humans, we have many dots in common. The pictures are very similar, but too often the dots remain unconnected. The commonalities unappreciated.

They Went

They were not perfect men
or women.
But they went.
They had flaws.
They were not all fighting
for our freedom.
But they went.
And many
did not return.

Some were jerks.
Some were assholes.
Some were angels.
And they went.

And when they returned
some had families
some had lives
many had nothing.

But they went.

They took their place on the line
so that others would not have to.

If I could, I would shake
the hand of each of them.
Because they went.
But I cannot.

   —Graves 5/27/13

Michael Graves

Love Match

To us, it was a game.

Immortal then
twenty and nineteen, and drifting.
Passing life at breakneck speed.

I wrote
and lived for music.
She captured the world
on film.
A skater, her blades carved
my dreams.
And from those carvings, came songs.

And we studied.
And we played
in tandem on a blissful run behind
the Gates of Eden.

Our life was chess, and chess is life
(less, of course, the unexpected change of rules by pieces.)

Every night
at dinner—two alone
in a noisy, crowded, college cafeteria.

Our board and
our armies of 16, we sat
eye-to-eye,
blue to brown
joined at the board.
A different plane.

Conversing in moves.

Pawns advancing
one step
at a time
to meet pawn.

Slowly savoring
each move.
Making the most of
the erotic pavane.
She'll "take" on a diagonal—
or from behind if the other is quick enough
to pass.
A slow mover, but transcendent
in the tango of the end game.

King's knight is prancing.
Out early.
Cutting corners to get to
The Show.
Moving in all directions
hoping to get some
satisfaction.
Flashy riding.

Queen's knight charges
recklessly in and out
defending all, at once
from every corner.

Cool and distant
she claims, to the end
until she, too
in heated lust of battle
is captured.

The tall bishop
with his heady crown
always waiting. Always yearning.
Poised for the incisive
long
diagonal
strike.

Michael Graves

Rooks trembling with eagerness to escape
their defending pawns
and get some action of their own.
Always the escape artists.
But once only.

The nimble way she used
her knights
enthralled me.
Her lascivious look as queen took bishop.
Positioning—always positioning
in the dance.

For an all too short nine-month eternity
we waged.

Until at last
I looked up from life.
With a flash of crystal insight.
And saw the sprite across from me
commanding an army.
She castled.

And I was left.
Downed king and empty chair.
And the game.

Too fragile to last
too tough to be forgotten.

No chance of mate.

   —Graves 1/1/15

Notes:
"Gates of Eden" is a reference to Bob Dylan's song "The Gates of Eden", which was written about the time that he spent in college.

Just Because

It's easy to write about grief.
About loss.
It's as easy as falling.

Weeping, after all, is not necessarily bad.
People weep
from loss, or from a feeling of relief.
People weep from pain or from a flood
of enhanced belief.

Grief is a well-traveled poetic road.
The sights to see along the way
are published in flimsy little brochures
for tourists to cram into their luggage
and discard once they get home.

I'm not saying that poetry
should (necessarily) be about
the beautiful songs of soaring angels.
Or about massive formations
of glowing clouds in a summer evening sky.

Far be it from me
to tell you
what to write.

It's my opinion.
Just because
it is.

Poetry's holy calling
is to stretch beyond the confines
of a comfortable mind.

To travel to that place beyond
sight.

Michael Graves

That place where dreams play out as real.

Because it's poetry.
> —Graves 10/17/15

Thanksgiving

Today, I am thankful.

For the rocky coast; the
challenging wind; the
circumstance that
makes me grow.

For the stars
which bid my vision
up and out.

For family, who warm my way
guide my steps
and make me a little
crazy, sometimes.

For friends, who
sweeten my life
with affinity.

For the one that I've
finally found, who
brings my life full circle.
And for falling in love
all of those times before.

For the child, who wakes
in the clear morning light
and is not afraid to see.
Who dresses the future
in dreams; and
graces the world
with wonder
and possibility.

Michael Graves

For those who make the music that
fills up spaces, in booming
joyous abandon, or peacefully sings
the sparkling stars to sleep
in the night sky.

For the poet
whose words blaze with dreams, that
inflame imaginations, kindle passions, stoke
the heat of life; and who paints with
rippling colors in the imagination
the road that takes us where
we have not been.

For the painter
whose vision spans the distance
between each of the separate
viewpoints of mankind
and joins them as one.

For the song defiantly sung, despite
suppression, and for those with
the courage to carry
the tune.

For those who walk
the lonely road
and keep the peace.

For the seekers of truth
and the dreamers of dreams
who return with visions
that seed the future.

For the clear, strong voice
which bends back lies with
simple truths, and drives out evil
like chaff before the summer wind.

Reflections on a Crystal Wind

That voice which vows to
never accept defeat.

And I am thankful for
those who come back.
They who are the
unstoppable
children of the wind.

And I am thankful
for those who share these thoughts.
Whoever you are
in whatever land
by whatever tongue
in whatever time.

For we share the same path.

   —Graves 11/19/15

Michael Graves

On Poetry (Art) and Social Responsibility

Poetry is one of the most dangerous, most powerful, and one of the most unorganized forces in the world.

Consider the effect that a single poet can create on the human psyche.

Shakespeare, Rumi, Rimbaud, Dylan, Poe, Pound, Dickinson, Baudelaire, Cummings, Neruda, Yeats, Plath, Ginsberg, Burns, Bukowski, Dylan Thomas, Blake, Frost, Wordsworth, Whitman, and countless others.

Poetry combined with music was powerful enough to play an important part in helping to change the social face of my country in the 1960's. If you were there to witness it, you know exactly what I mean. One of the most famous pieces of poetry of that decade begins: "How many roads must a man walk down/ before you call him a man..."

Poetry soothes the aching heart. It kindles the flame of love. It is a precursor to inspiration. It calls men to sail a sea that they otherwise might not. Poetry performs a catalytic function between conditions: a bridge between disassociation and engagement; between non-involvement and responsibility; between denial and consideration.

At some point, a piece of poetry left a mark on you that was indelible. You still can recall it. That quality in poetry can bring change to the world -- literally.

If poetry is not also used to bring about needed change in social and political conditions, it denies a fundamental aspect of its basic purpose, and to this degree and in this way, it lies fallow.

Poetry is not bound by physical barriers. It is not stopped by walls. It can infiltrate elitist compounds, and pierce the walls of fortresses and prisons. It can bypass embargoes as easily as a breeze travels down a city street. I am writing from a redwood forest in California. You are reading this. Distance is not a barrier to poetry.

One of the reasons that poets are held in contempt by those who use force to suppress, is that while poets command the very, very real skills to inflame the spirit of those who are oppressed and move them to active social change or even open, violent revolt; that ability is far too often used by poets for nothing beyond introverted maunderings, voiced in cautious, hushed, whiny tones. As a result, suppressors find spitting on poets a very safe thing to do.

Poetry is powered by the human spirit. It is carried in the hearts and minds of the people. Historically, ideas have toppled empires. All social movements—all of the changes in history—have been sparked by communication.

"...I am the song on the lips
of slaves.

I am sire to the million whispers in the night;
before the riotous dawn.

I am the throbbing life blood;
the hope that breathes yet, beneath the heel
of the iron boot.
And awaits its time.

And I am that time,
which will come.

I am the driver of men, beyond broad, deadly
expanses, thirsting
for new worlds.

I am the line
plotted past the edge of charts.

I am the dreams beyond those
yet dreamed.

Michael Graves

I am the new voice of songs yet
to be formed on the lips of
those yet to be born.
And I am the dawn
of a new Age..."

Poetry once lacked the proper distribution system. We now have a distribution system which is more powerful than any in the history of Earth—the Internet. Change can now potentially take place "one reader at a time" on a very, very broad scale. Poetry does not need to sway six billion people in order to achieve its goal. It only has to reach and affect those with significant influence, or reach a significant number of people, for change to occur.

What if we had a million poets creating life-changing pieces in a wave which is directed at a single point of oppression? Or directed at a focused, few points of suppression? Think about it. What kind of effect might we then create?

It is time to send the tyrants screaming into the night, pursued by a wave of voices that no number of bullets can ever kill.

Poetry can change the world. But only if it is wielded, not proffered. Get organized. Pass it on.

"Night Must Fall on the Regime"

The time has come.

Night must fall on the regime.

The summer air half a world away is filled
with the screams of souls that you have betrayed.

You, whose proper function is to serve.

You, who turn your country on the roasting spit of oppression,
charring humanity to black flakes over
the painful fires of violence; seasoned
with the smell of fear.

Reflections on a Crystal Wind

This is not the way of humanity!

You do not speak for me!
You could once commit your perverted crimes shrouded in secrecy.
But now, worldwide
awareness of your atrocities is just a URL click away.

And thus, is the bright light of day!
And thus, is the television camera!
And thus, are the kleig lights of the world stage!

The video taken with the phone of
the man in the street—upon whose neck
you once could stand with impunity
—and posted to the web, makes

secrecy no longer your option.
No longer your shield.

To sit silent and do nothing while you continue, degrades me and stains each of my brothers and sisters with shame.

To permit you to persist, reduces the humanity of each one of the inhabitants of Earth.
Each one.

This is NOT the way of a leader.

This is not the way of humanity.

A populace is NOT your collection of personal toys
to be played with, and bled!
You pathetic, wanton child!
There is no pride in this.
Only decrepitude.

Stalin was thus.
Hitler was thus.
George III was thus.
The Masters of the Inquisition were thus.

Michael Graves

These are your brothers-in-spirit.

If the only reasoning that you will respond to
is a knife at your throat,
then consider that you are now on notice.

Your lies and deceit will birth the bloody tumult.

I weep for your countrymen.
I weep for my brothers and sisters.

It is time.

Night must fall on the regime.

I am the poet.
And I live in a billion minds.
We are the dreamers of dreams.
And we will prevail.

Your remains will blow away on the fresh winds of morning
before the rising sun of a new day.

There are a million voices waiting to take my place.
A million songs being honed.
A sky-full of razor-sharp arrows that are all aimed at your heart.
Our songs live in the minds of your people.
Our songs form the million whispers in the night
before the riotous dawn.

Our songs feed the throbbing life-blood of hope
that breathes yet beneath the heel of the iron boot.
Awaiting its time.

And that time has come.

For the sake of humanity.
For the sake of songs yet to be formed
on the lips of those yet to be born.

Night will fall on the regime.

Reflections on a Crystal Wind

You cannot dull my advance.
Your suppression only sharpens
my quill and broadens my legend.

We live as one unturnable wave of forward motion.
And we speak for humanity.

We will outlive you.
We will outlast you.
You who would crush all hope.

You are my enemy.
This is personal.

I am the singer of songs.
I am the dreamer of dreams.
My brothers and sisters and I inspire the future, and craft
the inspirational blade that even now thirsts for your throat.
There are more poets on Earth than you can count.
And more than you can ever crush.

You cannot stop us.

The time has come.
Night will
fall on the regime.

> —Graves 2/11/15
> *"On Poetry and Social Responsibility"*

Author's Note:
Though this piece was originally written about poetry, its premise applies to all forms of art and the artists that power them. We are all in an unprecedented position to influence not only our culture, but the combined cultures of the planet. And who better to do it? Politicians have been wearing this hat for millennia and have driven themselves as a group into a generally distrusted and despised condition of existence. It is only fitting that we, as artists, bypass and handle. Not as those who would govern the culture, but as those who illustrate the

direction that a culture should properly take in its evolution from the existing scene to a more ideal scene, and provide effective encouragement and motivation for the achievement of that evolution. As artists, its our job and should be our united purpose.

About the Author

A West Coast Poet, Michael Graves has spent the past two decades living in a redwood forest in Northern California. His unusual approach to poetic subjects spans the spectrum from the cerebral to the deeply erotic and has won the hearts of thousands of online readers. "Reflections on a Crystal Wind" is his much anticipated foray into the realm of "offline" literature.

According to Graves, he began writing poetry in "self defense" in high school, "... in order to survive geometry class. My instructor was a great guy who was cursed with a droning, monotone speaking voice. So I started writing poetry in self-defense, to stay awake."

It wasn't until he took a poetry class with James Doyle in the mid-1970's, at the University of Northern Colorado, that he began to understand quality as it relates to poetry. "Among other things, Jim helped me to see that if I couldn't express an idea in a way that was different than it had been said before, why bother? Around that time I began the process of growing up, as a poet. I owe him a lot in that regard."

Graves says that he writes most of his pieces, "along lines of poetic reasoning which give the reader a positive experience, either emotionally or intellectually." He's had readers write and tell him that his poetry has helped them get through a difficult time. And in more than one case, he's been told it prevented a suicide."

Graves has been a business consultant since 1984, working mostly with small healthcare practices: "Practice owners bring me their dreams: Dreams that are not working. They are trying to help people, and something is preventing them from doing this. They tell me what they would truly like to accomplish, and

I show them how to achieve their dreams. I feel privileged to have this as my 'day job.' It also allows me time to write. For me, it doesn't get any better than that."

www.ingramcontent.com/pod-product-compliance
Lightning Source LLC
LaVergne TN
LVHW041338080426
835512LV00006B/521